The Song of the Thorns

Oh, thorns that sing a prickly tune,
They raise a ruckus 'neath the light of the moon.
With each small poke, they join in cheer,
Singing songs that make you fear!

Yet laughter bursts from every barbed note,
As woodland creatures all begin to gloat.
A jab, a jab, oh isn't it grand?
The finest jest in this wild band!

Whispers Under the Canopy

In shady nooks where secrets play,
The leaves chuckle in a breezy sway.
A squirrel's chatter adds to the fun,
As sunlight dances, everyone's on the run.

With tangled branches like old friends,
They poke and prod till the laughter bends.
A tickle here or a brush there too,
In the chatter of woods, the mischief grew!

Original title:
Ballads of Brambles

Copyright © 2025 Creative Arts Management OÜ
All rights reserved.

Author: Lila Davenport
ISBN HARDBACK: 978-1-80567-425-2
ISBN PAPERBACK: 978-1-80567-724-6

Sonnet of the Rugged Paths

Beneath the steps of sturdy shoes,
The brambles giggle, making their dues.
A tumble here, a stumble there,
They jest and tease without a care.

The bushes lean with a cheeky grin,
Inviting all to join their spin.
With every scratch from thorns so sly,
You'll laugh aloud, oh my, oh my!

Echoes from the Wildwood

In the wildwood where the oddballs roam,
A raccoon searched for his lost shiny comb.
"Have you seen it?" he asked with a frown,
While the badger just chuckled, "You'll never live it down!"

A chipmunk proclaimed, "I'm the fastest sprinter!"
But tripped on a root and fell in a splinter.
With a flick of the tail and a puff of his chest,
He laughed it off, "Still better than the rest!"

In a hollow log, a frog took the stage,
With a croak and a leap, he captured the age.
"Watch me hop like a superstar bright,
But wait—where's my band? They're out for the night!"

Yet in the chaos of fun, they found grace,
As the laughter kept bouncing in this woodland space.
Each twist and each turn was a dance on the floor,
Making memories that spirits adore!

Fables of the Thorns

In a garden bright and lush,
Sat a crow with quite a crush.
He chased lilies, tripped on thorns,
Wore a crown of silly adorns.

The daisies laughed, they'd never seen,
A crow who danced, a sight so keen.
With each step, he stumbled and swayed,
In the patch where mischief played.

But one day, in search of treats,
He bumped into prickly sweets.
A berry bush, he thought so kind,
Yet left him stuck, in vines entwined.

So, take heed if you roam about,
Not every bush is worth a shout!
For laughter comes with minor scrapes,
In the land of thorny shapes.

Whispers Under the Canopy

In shady nooks where secrets play,
The leaves chuckle in a breezy sway.
A squirrel's chatter adds to the fun,
As sunlight dances, everyone's on the run.

With tangled branches like old friends,
They poke and prod till the laughter bends.
A tickle here or a brush there too,
In the chatter of woods, the mischief grew!

The Song of the Thorns

Oh, thorns that sing a prickly tune,
They raise a ruckus 'neath the light of the moon.
With each small poke, they join in cheer,
Singing songs that make you fear!

Yet laughter bursts from every barbed note,
As woodland creatures all begin to gloat.
A jab, a jab, oh isn't it grand?
The finest jest in this wild band!

Riddles of the Hidden Briars

In briars so coy, riddles are spun,
With puns so sweet, you'll think it's fun.
A jabbering bug has a tale to tell,
Of bramble myths, where mischief does dwell.

They twirl and twist in the evening light,
Flashing sharp smiles that give quite a fright.
Solve the riddle 'fore evening's done,
Or the jolly branches will claim their fun!

Reverie Beneath the Jagged Leaves

In the thicket, squirrels prance,
Chasing shadows, what a dance!
Bumblebees in funny hats,
Buzzing loud like silly chats.

Rabbits hide, then hop away,
Wishing for a brighter day.
Mice in stripes, a fashion craze,
Display their styles in leafy ways.

The owl chuckles, wise and sly,
Winks at the antics flying by.
While frogs croak a merry tune,
Underneath the playful moon.

Laughter echoes, branches sway,
Nature's jesters at their play.
In this woodland circus show,
Joyful hearts begin to glow.

The Forgotten Echo of the Woods

In the forest, tales are spun,
Of talking trees that love to run.
Whispers of a breeze run high,
Tickling leaves as they pass by.

The hedgehog wears a crown of twigs,
Dancing with the silly jigs.
While raccoons snack on pies of bark,
Underneath the moonlit arc.

Goblins hide with giggles spry,
Playing tricks that make you sigh.
A snail in boots takes his chance,
Limping forward in his dance.

Laughter rings through every glade,
With little mischief poorly made.
Forgotten echoes call us near,
In these woods, we shed a tear of cheer.

Chronicles of the Untamed Thicket

Once a fox with fluffy tail,
Claimed the thicket without fail.
He held court with skunks galore,
As wisecracks flew forevermore.

Snails on scooters, drifting slow,
Competing in a wobbly row.
And loons that croon in silly tones,
Make music from the living stones.

A hedgehog tried to steal the show,
With stories only he could know.
But he tripped and fell on his snack,
And laughed till tears rolled down his back.

In the thicket, tales unwind,
With every critter, joy you'll find.
Chronicles penned in twigs and vines,
Sharing laughter without confines.

Eulogy for the Lost Grove

Here lies the grove of cheeky trees,
That waved hello with every breeze.
A squirrel once threw a grand party,
With acorns mocked in such a hearty.

The owls wore glasses, thought it grand,
While mice debated the best band.
With every rustle, laughter bloomed,
In this place so snugly groomed.

But one day winds, they came to call,
And twirled the laughter, made it fall.
Yet memories linger, soft and bright,
Echoing joy in the twilight light.

So raise a toast with leaves so green,
To the fun we had in a world unseen.
Though the grove may fade from view,
In hearts, its giggles still ring true.

The Bramble's Broken Promise

In the garden, weeds did sway,
Bramble promised sunny play.
But thorns crept in, oh what a jest,
Now we fumble with every quest.

Laughter echoes, vines entwine,
Bramble's plan was just a line.
With tangled roots that clasp so tight,
We stumble, grin, 'twas worth the fight.

Melodies of the Dappled Shade

In the grove where shadows dance,
Bramble sings in merry prance.
Frogs join in with ribbits loud,
To serenade the lumbering crowd.

Squirrels chuckle, leaves applaud,
With every note, the brambles nod.
A beetle twirls, a caterpillar sways,
In the joy of their dappled days.

Beneath the Gloaming Boughs

Gloaming comes, the shadows creep,
Bramble whispers, "Time for sleep."
But no one dares to close an eye,
For mischief lurks, oh my, oh my!

A raccoon snickers, a posy bee,
In the hush, they create a spree.
Moonlight shimmers, laughter swells,
Bramble's tales are wild, it tells.

The Song of Reluctant Blooms

Flowers bloom but not so keen,
Bramble's humor in between.
"Are we lovely?" they do ask,
With petals bright but quite a task.

Giggles echo from nearby leaves,
Bramble teases, "Just believe!"
A dance of colors, shy and bold,
In a world where laughter's gold.

Whispers in the Thicket

Amidst the leaves where critters play,
A squirrel shares tales of the day.
He danced with a beetle, made him his friend,
But lost a nut—oh, how it did end!

The rabbit tried to leap so high,
He tripped on roots, oh my, oh my!
With a wiggle and a twist in the air,
He landed softly, without a care!

Under the bushes, a fox tells a yarn,
Of a chicken that thought it could charm.
But the farmer was sly and quick on his feet,
Now the poor hen's dreaming of a delicious treat!

While the owl hoots, "Who, who can blame?
All of us will play this silly game!"
So join the fun beneath the trees,
Where laughter flows with the softest breeze.

Tales Beneath the Thorny Canopy

In the shadows where the wild things thrive,
A hedgehog rolls fast, feeling alive.
With quills like armor, he zooms with glee,
Yet bumps a cactus—oh, poor dear me!

A lizard basking on a big, warm stone,
Found a fly whispering, "You're not alone!"
But the moment he snapped, it buzzed with fright,
"Catch me tomorrow, I'll give it a bite!"

Up in the branches, a parrot sings loud,
"I'm the best bird, come see my crowd!"
But a crow caws back, "What's that you say?
Your feathers are bright, but your tunes—no way!"

And so they banter past thorny vines,
With giggles and jests that toe the line.
In this merry mess, let's raise a cheer,
For the untold stories that bring us near!

Serenade of the Twisted Vines

The vines are tangled, twisted with flair,
A dancing worm claimed it, unaware.
He wriggled and jiggled, the leaf said, "Stop!"
As a wise old snail began to plop.

"Was it a waltz, or a tango you tried?
I've seen better moves by the water side!"
The worm just laughed, and took it in stride,
"My moves are my own, I'll dance with pride!"

A cricket chimed in with a tune, so sweet,
"Let's host a ball, beneath the full moon!"
With twinkling stars as the glittering light,
The critters all gathered for a musical night.

Through the shadows, joy echoed around,
Where laughter was plentiful, harmony found.
In the tangled embrace of the enchanted dark,
The serenade lingered, leaving its mark.

The Knotted Tale of the Foxglove

In the meadow, flowers chat,
A foxglove whispered, 'How about that?'
She tangled herself in gossip tales,
While dodging the bees and playful snails.

'This is my friend, Mr. Bumblebee,
He once tried to dance, just like me!
But he got stuck in a sticky bind,
Now he sings tunes, a little maligned.'

The daisies chuckled, petals aglow,
'We really must see this show!'
With the foxglove leading the way,
They found him stuck—it made their day.

So next time you see a flower or bug,
Remember the laughs, give 'em a hug.
For in gardens there's humor, that often sprout,
In knots of friendships, wrapped about.

Lament on a Leafy Ledge

On a ledge where leaves do sway,
A squirrel sighed, 'Oh what a day!'
With acorn dreams and shiny schemes,
He pondered life, or so it seems.

'Could I leap to that branch so fine?
Or should I stay, and whine and whine?'
The wind just laughed, it knew too well,
That every leap comes with a swell.

With a wiggle and twitch, he took a shot,
But landed right where he'd rather not!
In a bush that tickled and sighed,
The thorns just chuckled, 'What a ride!'

Now the squirrel knows, in every bid,
That life's a jump, then you might skid.
So laugh a little when plans go wrong,
For it's the flops that create a song.

The Thicket's Gentle Murmur

In the thicket, where shadows play,
A rabbit hopped, 'What a bright day!'
With a wiggle of nose and a scamper of feet,
He made friends with all, quite a treat!

'Oh how lovely, this place to roam,
With sunbeams dancing, it feels like home!'
But enter the hedgehog, in slow-motion crawl,
'Watch out!' he squeaked, 'Or you'll tumble, friend, fall!'

With a tumble, they tumbled, oh what a sight,
A rabbit, a hedgehog, a flurry of fright.
The thicket giggled, a whispering cheer,
'Join us in fun—don't mind your fear!'

So amidst all the brambles and playful shout,
There's laughter found when you turn about.
For every thicket, tangled and odd,
Holds giggles and grins, like a secret nod.

Echoes from the Wilderness

In the thicket where the bunnies play,
A hedgehog rolls in a clumsy sway.
The bushes giggle with a rustling tune,
As squirrels dance beneath the moon.

A butterfly sneezes, what a sight!
A cactus winks in the fading light.
The bushes hum with a ticklish breeze,
While a bear attempts to climb, but just wheezes.

Crickets strum on rusty strings,
While chipmunks plot their little flings.
Nature's jesters parade around,
In this wild, raucous battleground.

So come and join this jolly spree,
Where each plant has a joke, just like me.
In the echoes where laughter rings,
The wilderness has the best of things.

The Wild Symphony of Nature's Thorns

Amidst the thorns, a bird takes flight,
While a bear tries to dance, what a sight!
With blossoms swaying, full of cheer,
Nature's orchestra plays loud and clear.

A hedgehog serenades a shouting tree,
The bushes join in with wild glee.
Each creak and crack, a note in disguise,
As the sun grins wide, painting the skies.

The flowers chuckle, the moss beats drums,
While a sly fox snickers, here she comes!
A weasel leaps, in a playful trance,
Saying, "Let's waltz! It's time for a dance!"

In the wild symphony, we all partake,
With each prickly thorn, a joy to make.
It's laughter and tunes we will adore,
In this green concert, forever more.

Whispers in the Thicket

In the thicket whispers of mischief abound,
Where tangled vines make a jolly sound.
A rabbit cracks jokes, oh what a delight,
While a cactus teases, "I'm sharp but polite!"

The trees gossip about the sly raccoon,
Who moonlights as a dancer under the moon.
A squirrel remarks with a cheeky grin,
"Who pinched my acorn? Let the fun begin!"

Each rustling leaf tells a tale, a quirk,
As the shadows play hide-and-seek with the murk.
Crickets pitter-patter like speedy feet,
Winking at moths in a rainbow, so sweet.

So hear the whispers that tickle your ear,
In a world where laughter is loud and clear.
Embrace the thicket, join this delightful crew,
Where every moment is a joke waiting for you.

The Briar's Lament

Oh the briar sings of pricks and jests,
Of playful nicks and nature's quests.
With every thorn, a giggle grows,
As the sun dips low and the soft wind blows.

A fox trips lightly, nearly falls,
While a barbed rose whispers to the walls.
"Don't mind the prick!" it sings with glee,
"For every jab, there's a laugh, you see!"

The bramble's tale is spun with mirth,
As critters gather, a celebration of earth.
A hedgehog grins, "I'm spiny, it's true,
But come closer, and I might tickle you!"

So join the lament of the briar's cheer,
In the wild lid of laughter, all sincere.
For in every prickle, joy can be found,
In nature's comedy, so profound.

Fables from the Wistful Wicket

In a wood where the squirrels play,
A hedgehog tried to join a ballet.
He twirled and spun, oh what a sight,
But ended up lost in a bush all night.

A rabbit with shoes far too tight,
Declared he could hop to new heights.
He slipped on a root, in a comical fling,
And danced with a mole who could only sing.

The owl gave a hoot, quite bemused,
As frogs held a party, all raucously infused.
They sang about flies, and other small snacks,
While a turtle believed he could dance on his back.

So listen, dear friends, to this tale of delight,
Of creatures who laugh until the moonlight.
For nature's oddities and quirks we adore,
In a world where fun's just outside your door.

Murmurs of the Wandering Wood

In a glade where the daisies all giggle,
A skunk tried to dance, and oh how it wiggled!
The rabbits all laughed at his funky display,
As he rolled on the ground in a fragrant ballet.

A parrot flew in, with a bright, cheeky grin,
He started to chatter about all his kin.
But tripped on a twig, and fluttered away,
Landing right next to a cow having a stay.

The cow told a joke about hay and the rain,
Which made all the critters burst into strain.
The chipmunks were chuckling, they fell in a heap,
As the sun set softly, they brushed off their sleep.

So wander, my friend, through this whimsical place,
Where laughter and fun keep a smile on your face.
In the murmurs of nature, a jest can be found,
In the wandering wood where chuckles abound.

The Coils of Nature's Tangled Song

There once was a fox with a marvelous tale,
Who thought he could sing, but only howled pale.
The owls rolled their eyes, and the badgers all scoffed,
As the trees swayed along, giving him a soft hoof.

A rabbit in glasses was reading a book,
He looked up and said, 'Now that's quite a crook!'
The fox took a bow, with a smile so wide,
While the hedgehog just snorted and stood back with pride.

The hedgehog then joined in, his voice low and sly,
With a tune so peculiar, you'd think he could fly.
The birds all cheered with their beaks in the air,
While the sun turned to giggles, a luminous flare.

So grasp these sweet moments, so tangled yet sweet,
In coils of laughter, life's rhythm we meet.
For nature sings softly, in quirky delight,
Creating a symphony of fun every night.

Portrait of the Wayward Stem

Once a stem decided to roam,
Jumping fences far from home.
With a wink and a twist of fate,
Found itself at a berry state.

Bouncing soft on a playful breeze,
Chased by ants with surprising ease.
Sipping dew from a morning cup,
Wiggled and giggled, never gave up.

Whispered tales to the nearby leaves,
Promised adventures on wild eves.
In a patch where the sun loves to shine,
Pitched a tent with friends, feeling divine.

Wanderlust in the roots so deep,
Spinning stories, never to sleep.
Oh, the fun beneath leafy booths,
The wayward stem chasing lost truths!

The Bramble's Enchantment

In the thicket, where mischief thrives,
A bramble danced, with daring dives.
Its thorns gave hugs, a prickly tease,
Luring critters with laughter and ease.

It conjured spells from vines so bold,
Told of gnomes with secrets untold.
Frogs in tuxedos croaked in delight,
A jamboree that lasted all night.

The moon peeked through, wearing a grin,
As squirrels joined in, twirling with spin.
With berries that sparkle like diamonds rare,
The bramble created a festive air.

But be wary, oh friends, of the charm,
For tangled feet might bring alarm.
Yet once caught in its whimsical plight,
You'll laugh and dance till the morning light!

A Chorus of Wildflowers

In a meadow where wild things play,
Flowers sang of a sunny day.
Petals swayed in a breezy trance,
Inviting bees to join the dance.

"Oh dear daisies, why so bright?
Your sunny faces bring pure delight.
Join us here for a vibrant spree,
Whirling petals, wild and free!"

With a pop, a blossom took flight,
Twirled about, in sheer delight.
Rosemary giggled, lavender chuckled,
As daisies whirled, their colors buckled.

In this tune of wind and bloom,
The laughter chased away all gloom.
Come celebrate in nature's tune,
Where wildflowers dance beneath the moon!

Retracing the Twisted Roots

A gnarled root, with tales so wild,
Rambled off, like a playful child.
Back through meadows, tangled and spun,
Searching for where the laughter's begun.

With a twirl and a bounce, it did roam,
Vowing to find its way back home.
Through thickets, they giggled and laughed,
While the wise old oak wood welcomed their craft.

"Where do we go?" the roots would ask,
In search of joy, a curious task.
Each twist and turn opened a door,
Showing treasures they'd longed for before.

So the roots danced in merry delight,
Chasing the sun, avoiding the night.
In the game of life, they found their place,
Retracing their steps in a joyous embrace!

Chronicles of the Gnarled Branches

In a forest where the twigs do dance,
A squirrel took a daring chance.
He leapt from wood to splintered thorn,
And laughed at roots that were quite worn.

The branches twisted, full of cheer,
A raccoon grinned from ear to ear.
With nuts behind his funny ear,
He swayed the branches, drank a beer!

The frogs joined in, they croaked a tune,
As petals swayed beneath the moon.
In brambles thick, they'd stomp and prance,
Creating quite a wild romance.

The gnarled tree gave a hearty groan,
As critters laughed, they felt at home.
With branches swinging, oh what a sight,
A merry jangle came with the night.

Melodies of the Tangle

In a thicket where the thorns do jive,
A hedgehog caught the rhythm alive.
With tiny feet he tapped in time,
To music made from a twisted vine.

Beneath the brambles, fleas would dance,
Each spindly twig gave them a chance.
A beetle hummed, a bumblebee buzzed,
Creating chaos that surely was fuzzed.

The snails in shells had quite the groove,
Each slow-motion twirl made them move.
They sped up slow, then slowed down quick,
With laughter loud, oh what a trick!

With friends entangled, a party indeed,
From frayed edges, they'd all take heed.
In funny shapes the shadows played,
In wild, tangled laughter, they all stayed.

Verses from the Shadowed Grove

In the grove where shadows tease the sun,
A cactus cactus on the run!
He joked with weeds, all sprightly and green,
While wiggling branches made quite the scene.

A parrot perched, with voice so loud,
Called forth the critters, a lively crowd.
With each brave joke, the boughs would sway,
Tickled by laughter that led the way.

Under dark canopies, shadows would loom,
While dancing fireflies lit up the gloom.
The giggling leaves swayed to the beat,
As owls hooted silly, in funky retreat.

In shadows deep, the fun never ceased,
Each twist of a limb made laughter increased.
A gnarled old tree claimed it was wise,
But in the chaos, it just rolled its eyes.

Ballads of the Wandering Vines

Oh, the vines that roam, quite a crazy sight,
They loop and twirl, a wild delight.
They travel far, through muck and mire,
Creating laughter, never tire.

With clinging hands, they hold on tight,
To everything that's in their sight.
A bumblebee buzzed, said, "What's this mess?"
The vines just twinkled, in playful stress.

They wrapped 'round trees with graceful flair,
Ignoring all the branches' glare.
"Let's swing and sway!" the bold vines cried,
While frogs leapt high, in joy they tried.

In tangled knots, they found their cheer,
As giggles echoed, loud and clear.
The wandering vines had tales to share,
With funny friends everywhere!

The Enigma of Thorny Trails

In tangled paths, we prance and sway,
A cactus dance, come join the play!
With sneakers stuck in thorns so tight,
We laugh at woes, punctured delight.

A hedgehog grins, he's quite a chap,
He rolls around, a spiky nap.
"No roadmaps here!" he calls with glee,
"Let's plunge ahead, come follow me!"

Through bushes thick, we take the chance,
Each branch a partner in this dance.
With every trip, we learn to jest,
For prickly paths are simply best!

So if you wander, heed this call,
Embrace the bumps, and have a ball!
The trails are thorny, laughter's key,
To navigate this comedy.

The Hoarse Call of the Bramblebird

A bramblebird sings, quite off the tune,
His voice a croak beneath the moon.
He chats with bees, they buzz and flee,
"Oh what a crooner!" they plea with glee.

He flaps his wings, just like a show,
Perched on a thorn, a flamboyant crow.
With every note, the thorns do sway,
The garden's stage, in disarray!

"Please stop!" the flowers beg in fright,
"For every squawk, you make us white!"
But bramblebird shrugs, and starts anew,
A comedic act, for all to view.

So tip your hats, and laugh out loud,
To our feathered friend, proud and loud.
His hoarse, wild calls, no greater thrill,
In thorny concerts, we cheer and chill!

Silhouettes in Greenery

Amidst the leaves, shadows do play,
Giggling figures, come out and stay.
A squirrel pretends to take a bow,
While dandelions dance, just like a cow.

In the brambles, secrets are shared,
With every whisper, laughter is flared.
A rabbit hops in a fashion absurd,
Claiming he's king, the bramblebird heard.

The thorns are crowns, we wear with pride,
In this jolly realm, let worries slide.
Beneath the green, mischief unfolds,
As silly tales and whimsy molds.

So gather around, let stories spin,
In the thickets where silliness wins.
Each silhouette frolics, bold and free,
In this bramble scene, come laugh with me!

Whispers of Pollen and Thorn

In breezy whispers, jokes take flight,
Pollen giggles, oh what a sight!
A bee buzzes in a frantic race,
"Stop tickling me!" in floral embrace.

With every bloom, a chuckle shared,
Their colors bright, their laughter bared.
Thorns poke fun, a playful snare,
While petals flutter, float in the air.

"Let's host a ball," the daisies shushed,
"Bring your best twirls, no need to rush!"
But thorns replied, in gruff delight,
"Watch your step, this jest's a bite!"

So join the spree, the pollen parade,
A party where laughter's never delayed.
Through the bramble's whimsy, twirl and yawn,
In the garden of mirth, till the break of dawn!

Secrets of the Hidden Grove

In the grove where whispers play,
Clumsy critters frolic each day.
Squirrels juggling acorns around,
Chasing shadows, they tumble down.

Tickling leaves with their tiny feet,
Jumping high, oh what a feat!
Mice on roller skates, oh dear,
Such a sight that brings us cheer.

A raccoon wears a hat quite grand,
As he leads a conga band.
The owls hoot in rhythmic fun,
Underneath the dazzling sun.

Every nook a giggle found,
Echoes of laughter all around.
In this grove where secrets thrive,
Nature's jesters come alive.

The Enchanted Snare

In a thicket thick and bold,
Bramble traps a tale untold.
A hedgehog caught in a clever net,
Squeaking loud, he's quite upset!

Nearby, a rabbit hops with glee,
Dancing round like it's a spree.
"Help me out!" cries Mr. Spike,
But the rabbit just avoids the hike.

"Why not join me, it's not so bad!
Adventure waits, don't be so mad!"
With a shrug, that hedgehog smiled,
Who knew being trapped could be so wild?

So they rolled through the snare and played,
Making magic, no plans delayed.
In a tangle, they found their song,
In the bushes where they belong.

The Palette of Bramble Roses

Petals covered in morning dew,
Colors bright in a floral brew.
Bees buzzing with a cheeky grin,
Painting skies where giggles begin.

A cheeky snail, he slides and glides,
On a leaf where laughter hides.
"Look at me!" he calls aloud,
As friends gather, so very proud.

Butterflies in a swirling dance,
Flap and flutter, a lovely chance.
Each brush stroke a whimsical turn,
Friendship's colors brightly burn.

"Oh what mischief in this place!
Let's mix hues and showcase grace!"
With every smile, the blooms anew,
In this palette of joy, we grew.

Chorus from the Choked Path

On the path where weeds do tread,
Sings a chorus, a funny spread.
A crew of bugs with hats so bright,
Hold a concert under moonlight.

Crickets chirp, a bass so low,
While fireflies put on a show.
"Twirl and spin!" the beetles cheer,
As giggles echo, spreading cheer.

"Join us now!" a ladybug sings,
In the yard of peculiar things.
Dancing leaves join in delight,
As the choked path shines so bright.

With laughter rolling, the stars align,
In a joyous, tangled twine.
A melody of fun and glee,
On each note, a memory.

The Mystery of Woven Roots

In a tangle of roots, they did dance,
Squirrels beheld, with a curious glance.
The hedgehogs giggled in soft little tones,
While thistles played cards with the acorns' phones.

A rabbit named Charlie lost all his bets,
To a wily old fox who had fouled his nets.
'Next time,' he sighed, 'I'll bring my best hat,'
But the hat was too small for a bunny like that.

The mushrooms joined in, with a jig on their caps,
Giggling and wiggling, a chorus of snaps.
'What's the prize for this grand little show?'
'Leftover carrots!' they tossed with a glow.

And so they all laughed in the roots' great embrace,
As laughter spread wide through that tangled place.
A mystery woven through laughter and cheer,
In the land of the bramble, nothing to fear.

Requiem for the Undergrowth

In the shaded glen where the wild things play,
The grass sang a tune that led many astray.
A fox lost his glasses while searching for food,
And a rabbit proclaimed, 'This is quite the mood!'

The ferns held a party with cucumbers served,
While snails made the rounds, feeling quite preserved.
'I'll have my salad with dressing,' they cried,
As the daisies rolled in, all decked out with pride.

The ants brought their trumpets, a raucous affair,
While fireflies twinkled in the evening air.
Yet one squirrel forgot which folk song he'd learned,\nAnd played on a leaf, so the forest just turned.

Thus echoes the story of laughter and fun,
As shadows grew long and day started to run.
The undergrowth hummed with quirky delight,
In the waves of the twilight, they danced till the night.

Ode to the Bramble's Embrace

Oh bramble so hearty, so prickly and bold,
You hide all your secrets and stories untold.
With berries so sweet, you make quite a scene,
While birds in your shadows sing songs evergreen.

A rabbit once boasted, 'I've gnawed on your vines!'
But the bramble just chuckled, 'I hold the best brines.'
The hedgehogs then joined in with a delightful skit,
While a sneaky old snail made off with a bit.

Leaping from branch to a bright summer note,
Came hedgehogs on scooters, quite ready to gloat.
'This is my kingdom, your thorns don't scare me!'
Declared Missda toads as they cheered with glee.

So here's to the bramble, a riddle so spry,
In the laughter and chaos, we happily sigh.
Together we frolic, no worries around,
In this realm where the quirks of the wild are found.

Secrets in the Green Wilderness

In the depths of the woods where the moss grows tall,
A raccoon named Timmy devised a great call.
He whispered of secrets held deep in the trees,
While ants danced around him, all swaying with ease.

The whispers of willows told amusing tales,
Of owls that wore glasses and crafted their sails.
The spiders brewed tea in their silk-spun abodes,
And shared laughter and crumbs with the wandering toads.

A ferret then dropped in with a hat made of leaves,
Claiming to see all the tricks up his sleeves.
But the frogs just croaked back with a boisterous cheer,
Saying, 'We hear nonsense, but we love it here!'

So secrets abound in this land lush and free,
Where giggles and stories blend easily.
In the wilderness green, with its charm so vast,
A funny parade of surprises is cast.

Journals of the Wandering Thorn

In fields where thorns do dance and sway,
The wanderers trip, and they often stray.
Their giggles echo through the rough,
As brambles tickle, never tough.

With every twist and every turn,
They laugh at stings, for lessons learn.
Who knew the thicket held such jest?
A prickly party, nature's guest!

Some climb the hedges, some just fall,
Yet laughter rises over all.
For roots may tangle, and vines will twist,
But joy is found, you can't resist!

So join the fun, let thorns be found,
In dancing shadows, peace unbound.
A garden fair, with glee unfolds,
As wand'ring thorns spin tales of gold.

The Sorrowful Song of Hedgerows

Oh hedgerows draped in shades of green,
They weep for woes, but aren't too keen.
With murmurs soft, they tell their tales,
   Of critters caught in tangled trails.

   Once a rabbit tried to hop,
But got stuck fast, oh what a flop!
He kicked and squealed, a comic sight,
As hedges watched, their branches bright.

A hedgehog pondered, 'Should I help?'
Then snorted loud, and laughed like kelp.
"Dear friend, just wiggle, don't despair!"
   The thorns all chuckled in the air.

So sing the song of tangled woe,
In hedgerows where the laughter flows.
For sorrow here wears a wry grin,
   As nature's jesters twirl within.

Rhythms of the Frosted Fern

The frosted fern with icy tips,
Shivers lightly, then does flips.
As winds do blow and frolic by,
The fern gives in, and starts to fly.

With every gust, it twirls around,
A frosted ballet on the ground.
Graceful moves with a silly flair,
As snowy sparks dance in the air.

The ferns giggle with each spin,
For chilly days, they wear a grin.
'The colder, the better!' they jest,
As winter's chill puts them to test.

So celebrate this frosty dance,
Embrace the chill and take a chance.
For laughter blooms in wintry glee,
As ferns invite you—come and see!

The Gnarled Root's Secret

Beneath the moss, where secrets lie,
A gnarled root whispers, oh so sly.
It chuckles low, with every moan,
Of mischief planned, and jokes well-known.

'Oh, gather 'round!' it calls with glee,
'For I've a tale of mystery!
How critters trip on roots so grand,
And tumble down in woodland's band!'

A squirrel once tried to boast and brag,
But missed his mark and hit a snag.
The root erupted, laughter loud,
As woodland friends formed a crowd.

So heed this root, with wisdom vast,
For nature's humor is unsurpassed.
In gnarled embrace, let joy be found,
As laughter lingers all around.

The Tangle's Embrace

In the garden where weeds convene,
A cat tries to nap on a leafy green.
With thorns that poke and stickers that cling,
He dreams of life as a fluffy king.

The dandelions laugh at his furry plight,
As he wrestles with brambles, oh what a sight!
A tumble and roll, he gives quite a show,
The king of the garden, or so he'll decree so.

The Briar's Dance

In the evening glow, the bushes sway,
With a rustling tune for the critters at play.
A rabbit leaps high, but lands in a twist,
While the thorns bop around like they can't resist.

Then come the bees, with their buzzing beats,
Joining the brambles in whimsical feats.
With each little jig, the mischief expands,
A meadow of chuckles in nature's own bands.

Elegy for the Lost Petals

Oh little petals, where did you go?
You danced with the breeze in a vibrant show.
But a bramble, so sneaky, pulled you away,
And left just your memory to reminisce and sway.

The flowers now grieve, with laughter subdued,
For each little petal that bramble imbued.
But together they chuckle, in grieve they unite,
To tell tales of mischief through day and through night.

A Dancer in the Underbrush

In the thickets where no one will tread,
A squirrel's ballet spins overhead.
With jumps and twirls that knock down the thorns,
Creating a ruckus that's briskly adorns.

A hedgehog joins in, with prickles that shine,
And together they cloak the old oak in vine.
With giggles and squeaks, they twirl round and round,
The best little dancers that nature has found.

Song of the Thorned Boughs

In a forest thick with twists and turns,
Where every branch has lessons to learn,
A squirrel danced on a crooked vine,
Spinning tales of mischief, oh so fine.

"A hug from a bush? Oh, what a thrill!"
Cried the bird just tripped on a gnarled hill,
With every tumble and every fuss,
Laughter blooms 'neath the thorny bus.

A hedgehog strolled with a crown of spikes,
Thinking he's royal, as though he's on bikes,
But tripped on a twig, oh what a scene,
Waving his arms like a regal machine!

So here in the brims where the wild things play,
Silly dances chase the gloom away,
Each thorny joke whispers under the sun,
In this enchanted place, where we all have fun.

Echoes of Vines

The vine swung low, with a cheeky grin,
Inviting all critters to join in the spin,
A rabbit hopped, then stumbled in glee,
Cursing the vine, "Oh, why doesn't it see!"

With each twist and turn, the laughter would ring,
The lizard sighed, "What a foolish thing!"
"Don't blame the vine!" chirped a wise old bat,
"It's just what it is, a vine, fancy that!"

A deer tried to leap over a patch,
But the vines grabbed his feet like a mismatched catch,
"Take that, my friend, as you try for the crown,
Who knew that a weed could bring you down?"

Beneath the green canopy, fun never ends,
With giggles and joy, nature's dear friends,
In this tangled realm of the laughable lines,
Where whispers and echoes dance with the vines.

Serenade of the Wildwheat

In fields of wildwheat, the breeze brings a tune,
Where critters gather beneath the round moon,
The weasel pranced in elegant style,
With two left feet that could crack up a smile!

"Oh, toss me a seed, let me try for a dance!"
A chipmunk laughed, giving fate a chance,
But every hop had him bouncing around,
Tangled in laughter that echoed the ground!

The owls were hooting, "Now isn't this grand?
Each flip of the wheat creates quite the band!"
With whispers of joy through the bending stems,
The night became vibrant with giggles and gems.

So sway with the wild and laugh with delight,
For in this grassy stage, all is just right,
Beneath the soft starlight, the fun has no end,
In the serenade where all join to blend.

Shadows Beneath the Thorns

In the shade of the thorns, mischief does bloom,
A juggling raccoon summoned laughter and zoom,
With acorns and berries, he'd put on a show,
A circus of critters, all lined in a row!

"Oh look at that squirrel, an acrobat true,
Flip-flopping 'round like it's nothing to do!"
But tripped on a branch, what a comical sight,
As he tumbled and rolled, oh what pure delight!

The shadows danced, playing tricks in the night,
While giggles and chortles took flight in their plight,
A badger piped in, "This party's a blast!
Beneath these sharp thorns, we're having a blast!"

So here in the darkness, where shadows take flight,
And laughter blooms brightly, chasing off fright,
In the company of friends, we lighten our loads,
Where humor spins tales in the tangled roads.

The Thistledown's Caress

In a field where thistles sway,
Came a bee who lost his way.
He danced and twirled, oh what a sight,
Tickled by fluff that felt just right.

The thistledown laughed with glee,
As the bee fell, oh dear me!
He buzzed and hiccupped, quite a show,
Stumbling back to the flowers' glow.

A ladybug joined in the fun,
Sliding down on the bee's bum.
Together they spun, a floral whirl,
In the kingdom of petals, they'd twirl and swirl.

Oh, what a chase in nature's game,
Where nothing was ever quite the same.
With each silly tumble and dance,
The thistledown's kiss brought forth a trance.

Weavers of the Bramble's Fate

In the thicket where shadows play,
Eager spiders weave all day.
With threads like jokes, snagging the breeze,
They chuckle softly, aiming to please.

One little spider, quite the prankster,
Dared to dress up like a dancer.
With a mask made of leaves and a hat on top,
He spun a web, and oh, how he'd hop!

He caught a fly with a witty line,
"Join my party, you'll have a fine time!"
The fly just buzzed, then flew away,
Leaving the arachnid in dismay.

But laughter echoed in the glen,
The spiders knew they'd try again.
For in every twist, and every turn,
New chances for joy, they yearned to learn.

Whims of the Wandering Briar

There once was a briar with dreams to roam,
Sought the world beyond its home.
With spiky shoes and a curious peep,
It toppled down from the hill, far steep.

"Oh look at me!" the briar declared,
"Adventure awaits, I'm unprepared!"
It tumbled through brambles, like a rolling ball,
Chasing down flowers, giggling through it all.

A butterfly asked, "Where are you headed?"
"To places where giggles are truly threaded!"
The briar replied, "I've lost my way,
But I'm sure the sun will guide my play!"

With a playful bounce and a cheeky grin,
The wandering briar felt joy within.
For in its travels, it found delight,
In the quirks of nature, morning and night.

Twilight in the Bramble Patch

As twilight brushed the bramble patch,
Fireflies danced, oh what a match!
They twinkled like stars, in a merry way,
Turning the night into a cabaret.

A hedgehog wiggled, sporting a grin,
"Let's party folks, let the fun begin!"
With shadows as partners, they swayed and spun,
In the soft glow of dusk, under the sun.

A wise old owl hooted a tune,
Filled with laughter, bright as the moon.
"Don't be shy, join in the spree,
In the bramble's embrace, we'll all be free!"

So under the stars, they danced till late,
In the bramble patch, it was quite first-rate.
With giggles and warmth, they melted the night,
In a world of laughter, everything felt right.

Cacophony of Bramble Whispers

In the thicket where shadows play,
Bramble critters dance all day.
A hedgehog hums a silly tune,
While bumblebees buzz underneath the moon.

A squirrel juggles acorns with flair,
As rabbits tease with fluffy hair.
The branches giggle, and leaves clap loud,
In this woodland, we're all quite proud.

The thorns wear hats made of bright blooms,
And every corner has silly grooms.
With laughter echoing through the night,
Who knew brambles could bring such delight?

A fox in boots stumbles on his feet,
While badgers pull pranks, oh, what a treat!
Nature's jesters, so clever and spry,
In this forest, we're never shy!

Spirals of Thicket Dreams

In spirals where mischief thrives,
The brambles weave their playful lives.
A porcupine with a feathered hat,
Squeezes in tight, oh fancy that!

The rabbits debate whose ears are long,
While crickets tap to a jazzy song.
The twigs all groove, their rhythm's grand,
We sway along in this wild band.

A raccoon with cookies stirs the pot,
And everyone claims he ate the lot.
But in this mess, no one feels bad,
Just sharing treats makes us all glad!

From bushes bright with giggly smiles,
To prancing foxes in crazy styles,
The thicket dreams with laughter's thread,
In every nook, bright joy is spread!

The Briar's Heartbeat

In brambles thick, a heartbeat thumps,
A dance of shadows, wide-eyed jumps.
The thorns they wiggle, a prickly cheer,
While fireflies twinkle, so bright and near.

A squirrel breaks into a funny jig,
With wispy branches, he snags a twig.
The briar whispers secrets of glee,
As critters tumble and as they flee.

'Twas a badger's hat made from spent bark,
That started this party and lit the dark.
With laughter so loud, it caught the moon,
The briar's heartbeat sings a tune!

In the midst of this joyful spree,
A porcupine sings in high C.
So cheer for the thorns and their sprightly fun,
In the heart of the bramble, we bask in sun!

Underneath the Serpent's Shadow

Underneath where shadows creep,
Bramble tales begin their leap.
A snake in shades, so grand and sly,
Tells stories of a pie up high.

The hedgehogs giggle, rolling about,
While owls hoot in a raucous bout.
A turtle joins with quite a shell,
His slow dance casts a laughter spell.

With brambles thick, adventures grow,
As wily critters steal the show.
Each twist and turn brings goofy sights,
Under shadows, we dance through nights.

So if you wander, take heed, my friend,
In bramble lands, the fun won't end.
With smiles and games, we fill the air,
Underneath the serpent's stare!

Hymn of the Lonely Rose

In a garden full of cheer,
A rose woke up, feeling sheer.
With petals bright and thorny pride,
She strutted forth, a joyful ride.

The daisies laughed, oh what a sight,
"You're too prickly, dear, not quite right!"
But she just twirled and danced around,
While bees buzzed off with a silly sound.

A butterfly landed with dashed delight,
"Your thorns won't stop me, I'll take flight!"
But she giggled back, with a wink so sly,
"You'll need a band-aid if you fly too high!"

So here's to the rose, so bold and bright,
In a world where thorns bring a laugh, not fright.
She blooms with glee, a sight to see,
In her funny, proud, thorny jubilee.

Fragments of Twisting Vines

In the woods, where the wild things creep,
Twisting vines had secrets deep.
They laughed and joked, entangled tight,
Pulling squirrels into a funny plight.

A rabbit jumped, slipped, and fell,
"These vines are trying to build a spell!"
But the vines just chuckled, coiling fast,
"We're just here for some fun, make it last!"

They tangled a frog and a curious toad,
"Please don't hop here, this is our road!"
Yet the creatures laughed, grew bold with glee,
In the wild play of flora, they'd all agree.

So if you wander where twisters twist,
Join the laughter, you surely can't miss.
For vines that bind can also amuse,
In a funny forest, you can't refuse!

Tales Woven in Thorns

In a patch of thorns, tales took flight,
With whispers of gossip, both day and night.
The brambles chatted, oh what a scene,
Trading old stories, a gossip routine.

"Did you hear the tale of the clumsy snail?"
"He slipped on a leaf, oh what a fail!"
With every poke, a chuckle would bloom,
As they spun their yarns in the floral room.

A hedgehog chimed in with wit so quick,
"I once took a nap on a cactus thick!"
The thorns all giggled, growing quite wild,
In the bramble tales, no one was reviled.

So gather 'round when the thorns are alive,
For tales that dance and twist and strive.
In every prick lies a story to tell,
Of laughter and fun, in a thorny shell.

The Fable of Hidden Paths

On hidden paths where the brambles creep,
Lies a tale where giggly creatures leap.
A raccoon once lost his way in a thicket,
Tripped over branches in a curious wicket.

An owl hooted loud, in the moon's embrace,
"Just follow the giggles, you'll find your place!"
But the raccoon snorted, with mischief in mind,
"I'll find my way—if I'm not inclined!"

Through twists and turns, he stomped with flair,
Only to tumble into a snorting bear.
They both just laughed, in the thick of it all,
Making friends in the backwoods brawl.

So heed this fable, listen close, dear friends,
Follow the laughter where the fun never ends.
In hidden paths where the brambles sway,
You might just stumble on a brighter day.

Lament of the Briar Rose

In the garden, she did twirl,
A rose with thorns, such a whirl.
She danced with bees in delight,
But pricked her toe in the night.

The birds sang her sweet refrain,
While squirrels laughed at her pain.
"Oh, look at that silly bloom!"
"Getting stuck is her own doom!"

With petals bright and full of cheer,
She giggled, "Do not shed a tear!"
For each prick is just a game,
Life's funny, never the same!

So here's to the briar's jest,
A rose that truly passed the test.
With laughter bright in the air,
Life's pricks are silly and rare.

Rhapsody of the Unruly Thorns

Oh, thorns that dance in the breeze,
Causing chaos with such ease!
They poke the socks of passing folks,
And play at hide and seek with jokes.

A branch that tried to break a fall,
Just tangled up and hit the wall.
It shouted out, "Hey, who's to blame?"
As birds just chirped, "What a game!"

The fence grew weary of their pranks,
With every jab, it's lost in thanks.
"Stop pulling me into your mess!"
"Oh dear thorns, we must confess!"

Yet laughter spreads where thorns remain,
Their ruckus fills the air like rain.
For in each prick lies a soft smile,
They keep us laughing all the while.

Songs Among the Hidden Paths

Through tangled trails, the laughter soars,
With hidden paths, life has its scores.
A bramble bush sings a tune,
A melody bright under the moon.

"Watch your step!" the travelers cheer,
With thorns that beckon, "Come over here!"
Each foot that slips on a hidden root,
Turns into giggles, a joyful hoot.

The paths twist in ways quite absurd,
As wanderers trail off with a bird.
"Found a snail!" they exclaim in glee,
While brambles giggle, "Wait for me!"

In the shadows where secrets play,
The songs echo, come join the fray!
For in every prick, there's laughter found,
In hidden paths, joy is unbound.

The Enchanted Wood's Lament

In an enchanted wood, tales spin,
Where thorns like to sneak and grin.
The trees chuckle with every twist,
And thorns beckon with a playful whisk.

A hapless hiker found the way,
But met a thorny display.
"Navigating by the stars?"
"Oh dear, you'll need more than that to spar!"

Spiders weave webs of laughter near,
As branches poke with a grinning cheer.
"Watch your back!" the other trees say,
"For these pricks are here to play."

Yet, within this brambly nest,
The enchantment grows, at its best.
In every thorn, a story to tell,
Of woods where humor casts its spell.

The Secret Life of Brambles

In the garden, brambles dance,
Twisting, turning, at every glance.
They gossip low, oh what a tease,
Plotting schemes with the buzzing bees.

A leaf in one hand, a thorn in the other,
They giggle and wiggle like a silly brother.
"Let's trip the pruner!" they plot with glee,
"Oh, won't it be fun? Just you wait and see!"

Dancing vines with a twist and shout,
They lounge by the fence with a joyful pout.
"To wrap around ankles is such a delight,
We'll make every garden a whimsical fright!"

With laughter profound and mischievous flair,
Brambles unite in a wild affair.
A secret life full of jest and cheer,
In their tangle of fun, there's nothing to fear!

Reverie Amongst the Thorns

Beneath the sun, the thorns take a seat,
Wondering who might be their next treat.
They chuckle and jive with the rustling leaves,
"Here comes a squirrel, let's see if he grieves!"

With long, pointy fingers they wave hello,
While a chipmunk scurries, oh so low.
"Catch him! Don't let him nibble our snack!"
But the chipmunk is quick, and he's back to the pack!

In their patchy embrace, a crow makes its call,
"Your thorns are so sharp, dear, you should be enthralled!"
But the thorns just shrug, "We like to be bold,
And tell silly tales that never get old!"

Daisies present, as the brambles rejoin,
A jester's convention in the cidery groin.
With laughter and whimsy among the twine,
Their revelry thrives, and the sun starts to shine.

The Lark's Soliloquy in the Thicket

In the thicket where larks like to perch,
They crow 'bout the brambles and get quite the search.
"Dear thorns, you're a mess! A tangled-up scent,
Do you ever stop growing? You're ever so bent!"

With feathers a-fluff, they stand with disdain,
"Must you shoot your sharp spikes like a crazy train?"
But the brambles just giggle, "Come join in our play,
You're welcome to dance if you happen to stray!"

"Oh, what a circus," the lark starts to sing,
"Surrounded by thorns is a curious thing!"
And with a swift flap and a risqué ballet,
They knock over beetles and dance them away.

With the thorns as their stage, they all take a bow,
The performance of larks causes laughter and wow.
As the audience grows, in the thicket they'll dwell,
Celebrating thorns, oh, they're under their spell!

The Wilderness' Rhapsody

Amongst the woods where wild things grow,
The brambles unite to put on a show.
"Softly now, don't catch our guests unaware,
Let's twirl and let tumble every creature out there!"

With a rustle and rattle, they act like a tease,
"Who's creeping our way? Could it be that old tease?"
And with cheeks all a-blush, they wrap round a hare,
"Jump high if you dare! We promise, we swear!"

A squirrel named Chuck with an acorn in hand,
Finds himself stuck, it's a ruffled-up band.
"Oh, help me!" he shouts, fluttered and fraught,
But the brambles just giggle, "Oh, look what we've caught!"

With laughter like music, their rhapsody rings,
As creatures of chaos spread joy on their wings.
In the wild heart of nature, through thorns they will weave,
Creating a world where all can believe!

The Dance of the Thorned Whispers

In the moonlight, thorns take flight,
They jig and twirl, what a sight!
A prickly party on a bough,
Who knew they'd dance? Not me, somehow.

They poke their feet in playful grace,
Each sharp jab a little chase.
But watch your step, oh do take care,
For one wrong move might leave a tear.

The hedgehogs snicker, watch them prance,
"Who knew the thorns could love to dance?"
In the shadows, laughter grows,
As thorns tango beneath the rose.

So if you hear a rustling call,
It's just the brambles having a ball!
Join the fun, though do be wise,
Be careful, or you'll be their prize.

Legends of the Overgrown Hedges

In the depths of wild green thicket,
The shrubs conspire, oh what a racket!
Ghosts of gardeners long gone roam,
Lost in the brush, far from home.

They tell of berries that taught to sing,
And thorny vines that mimic spring.
A tale of brambles, bold and proud,
Who once held court, so loud, so loud!

The rabbits giggle, the squirrels sigh,
As tangled messes reach for the sky.
"Dear friends," they say, "take heed and listen,
These shrubs have dreams, and they glisten!"

So wander through this leafy maze,
And hear the legends of the bramble's ways.
With every twig, a story shared,
Of overgrown charms, and no one cared.

Hymn of the Forgotten Trails

Among the paths where no feet tread,
The thorns compose their ballad spread.
Each twist and turn, a note to sing,
Of hidden trails and nature's bling.

The critters gather, a lively crew,
"A hymn of the forgotten we shall pursue!"
With each scratched elbow, they bop along,
Making mischief, singing their song.

The mice swing low, the birds take flight,
Snagged by brambles, what a plight!
Yet laughter echoes, spirits soar,
Even the thistles join in with a roar.

So if you venture down this route,
Embrace the chaos, dance about!
For every scrape, a chuckle sound,
In the hymn of trails lost, joy is found.

The Briar's Embrace

In a garden where wild roses weep,
The briars beckon, secrets keep.
"Come closer, friend!" they sweetly hum,
But watch your toes, they'll make you glum!

A hug of thorns, a prickly greet,
"Just a kiss, now shuffle your feet!"
The roses giggle, petals aglow,
While the briars whisper, "You won't say no!"

"Oh, dear traveler, rest and stay,
We promise not to lead you astray!"
But as you sit, they tighten the hold,
With every chuckle, their embraces bold.

Yet shrieks erupt from the ladybugs,
"Save yourself from these thorny hugs!"
So if you're drawn to their sweet embrace,
Just know, my friend, it's quite the race!

The Gravelly Path's Soliloquy

Oh, the path is rocky, bumpy with care,
Each stone a dancer, twirling in air.
I trip and tumble, a sight to behold,
With laughter collected, my story unfolds.

The gravel cracks jokes, it chuckles a bit,
As I stumble and giggle, not daring to quit.
Each step is a riddle, each twist a surprise,
I swear it's a comedian, through all my replies.

Now trees join the jest, with their branches so fine,
They wave with delight, as if crossing a line.
A squirrel in a hat might tiptoe nearby,
While I, feeling fabulous, let out a loud cry.

Will I walk on this path till my laughter runs dry?
Or is it a comedy of missteps, oh my!
With each hiccup and blunder, a new tale I weave,
With the gravelly path, I shall never leave.

A Dream Amongst the Briars

In dreams of the night, I found myself stuck,
Amongst all the briars, what terrible luck!
Yet a hedgehog appeared with a wink and a grin,
Said, "Life's full of prickers; let's dance and spin!"

The thorns nodded knowingly, a wild, leafy crew,
They tossed out their berries, all sparkly and blue.
I tripped on a root, in a tumble so grand,
But laughter erupted—oh, isn't life planned?

With each prickly embrace, I learned how to sway,
And frolic with jests in the moonbeam's soft play.
The croaking of frogs sang our silly duet,
In a world of the brambles, I had no regret.

So here in the thickets, I twirled all night,
With stingy companions, all heavy with might.
A dream amongst briars turned grand and absurd,
As I whispered my secrets to every soft bird.

Revelations on the Thorny Trail

On the thorny trail, what glory I see,
A hedgehog is laughing, and so is the bee.
Their giggles echo, blending with the breeze,
As the thorns throw their arms, attempting to tease.

Each step a new puzzle, a quirkier quest,
I chuckle at nature's odd sort of jest.
The briars conspire, with tricks on their mind,
While I, elated, know laughter is kind.

A squirrel chimes in, dropping acorns like gold,
While I dodge in delight, feeling brave, feeling bold.
The path twists and turns, but oh what a sight!
As brambles all dance in the soft moon's light.

With each thorny embrace, a tale to bestow,
The secrets of laughter, I cherish and know.
On this whimsical trail, where humor prevails,
I find joy in the journey, no matter the gales.

The Wild Heart of the Meadow

In the meadow so wild, with daisies awash,
I stumbled on laughter, oh what a splosh!
The wind tickled grass as it danced with delight,
And I rolled in the petals till dusk took the light.

A rabbit appeared, all flamboyantly dressed,
He twirled on his toes, put my giggles to test.
With every wild hop and a silly old grin,
He declared, "Join the party, let the fun begin!"

As butterflies fluttered in curious loops,
I grasped at my sides, laughing loud with the troops.
The flowers chimed in with a colorful shout,
In this meadow of mischief, there's never a doubt.

So here in the wild heart, where all seem to play,
Every tumble and trip takes my worries away.
With daisies and laughter entwined in the sun,
I'll dance with the meadow until day is done.

www.ingramcontent.com/pod-product-compliance
Lightning Source LLC
Chambersburg PA
CBHW071839160426
43209CB00003B/350